STUDEBAKER LARK

1959-1966 PHOTO ARCHIVE

Ed Reynolds

Photo Archive Series

Enthusiast Books

www.enthusiastbooks.com

Library of Congress Control Number: 2003103545

ISBN-10: 1-58388-327-4
ISBN-13: 978-1-58388-327-3

Reprinted February 2018

Printed in The United States of America

Copyediting by Jane Mausser

COVER PHOTO: Original Studebaker factory photo of a 1962 Lark Deluxe 2-door sedan.

Acknowledgments

This book is dedicated to the thousands of Studebaker enthusiasts around the world who continue to resurrect, restore, drive, and enjoy these unique vehicles. Studebaker had an interesting history and it is perpetuated by enthusiasts keeping the marque alive.

Although the majority of photos in this book are from my own Studebaker photo collection, the material was enhanced by photos furnished by Richard Quinn.

Introduction

Studebaker nearly went out of business in 1956. The Eisenhower administration cooked up a management deal with Curtis Wright and gave them some military contracts in exchange for helping manage Studebaker-Packard. The company continued to struggle in 1957 and 1958 and Studebaker President Harold E. Churchill knew he needed to do something new. Studebaker couldn't compete with the Big Three because the playing field was inherently tilted. He needed a niche market that Studebaker could pursue without competition from the major auto companies. Making a smaller car was a logical conclusion. After all, American Motors was setting sales records with its less than attractive Rambler. Studebaker could do the same.

With a very limited budget and not much time to come up with a new car, development started late in 1957. In fact, it wasn't a new car. It was a major facelift of the 1953 Bob Bourke–designed sedan. It was the same chassis with an 8-inch section removed, the same roof except for some minor changes, the same engine and driveline, and the same basic dashboard. What *was* new were the front and rear fenders, hood, and front and rear panels. The result was a car that slightly resembled the previous model Studebaker, but also looked like a new car.

The car was kept simple to cut costs. Only five basic colors were offered, no metallic, and no two-tones. Front and rear bumpers were interchangeable. Power windows and seats were no longer offered. The cars went back to single headlights. Only two basic models were offered, the Deluxe and the Regal. Four body styles were available, the 4-door sedan, 2-door sedan, 2-door hardtop, and 2-door station wagon. Two engines were offered, the 170-cid flathead 6-cylinder and the 259-cid V-8. Each could be attached to a standard 3-speed, overdrive, or automatic transmission; all were operated from the steering column.

Lark sales were good for 1959. In fact, it was the best sales year the company had since 1950. Morale was up at the factory and there was a new short-lived optimism surrounding Studebaker. This optimism was short-lived because it soon became known that the Big Three automakers were also working on their own versions of smaller cars that would debut with their 1960 models.

Changes were few to the 1960 Lark. A slight change was made to the grille mesh, taillight lenses, and side stainless moldings. Some new colors were added but the biggest change was the addition of a convertible and a 4-door station wagon to the model lineup. As expected, sales dropped some in 1960, but it still was a pretty good year.

The 1961 model didn't look that much different than the 1959 or 1960, but it actually did have many changes. These changes included the roof, hood, trunk lid, nose panel and grille, taillights, dashboard, and front fenders. Oval steering wheels became standard in 1961 and continued through 1966. Dual headlamps were back on Regal models and a folding sunroof was added as an option. The "Cruiser" model was added; it had a 4.5-inch longer wheelbase that extended rear seat legroom. The Cruiser came with the 259-cid V-8 and the 289-cid

V-8 became available again in 1961 on this model. Another major change in 1961 was that an overhead valve 6-cylinder engine replaced the old Champion flathead that had been in service since 1939.

Studebaker was working at this time on two totally new cars that were to be introduced in 1962. One was to be a continuation of the Lark on the same 108.5-inch wheelbase. The other was to be on a smaller 100-inch wheelbase powered by a 4-cylinder, horizontally opposed, water-cooled engine.

Sherwood Egbert replaced Harold Churchill as Studebaker president in January of 1961. Egbert had previously headed McCulloch, makers of chainsaws. Egbert scrapped the two new design proposals, and hired Milwaukee industrial designer Brooks Stevens to do a facelift for the 1962 model. Stevens changed the roof, hood, nose panel and grille, front fenders, trunk lid, and taillights. Dual headlights were now on all of the Larks. The longer chassis previously used only on the Cruiser was made standard for all 4-door models. A new Daytona model was added as a hardtop or convertible with slightly different body side moldings and upgraded interiors over the Regal models. In May of 1962, a Lark Daytona convertible paced the Indianapolis 500-Mile Race.

Brooks Stevens also began working on some long-range plans for Studebaker. He had three prototypes built as styling studies for 1964, 1965, and 1967 models. The first was a 4-door station wagon, then a 4-door hardtop, and then a 2-door hardtop.

The 1963 Lark appeared very similar to the 1962 model, although the roof, windshield, and back glass were new. The grille mesh was changed along with the body side moldings. The back of the car had some added moldings too. The instrument panel was new and featured a vanity in place of the usual glove box. The big change in 1963 was the new station wagon model called the Wagonaire. The rear section of the roof slid forward allowing tall objects to be carried upright, or it could be left open for better ventilation. All station wagons came with the sliding roof but it could be deleted for $100.00 savings.

Studebaker debuted the Avanti in 1963 with its beefed up engines, both supercharged and nonsupercharged, as well as front disc brakes, a floor-operated automatic transmission, and heavy-duty suspension. These were all standard on the Avanti and became available in Larks. The intention of this new fiberglass sports car was to reshape the image of Studebaker and to attract buyers into the showrooms to buy Larks as well as Avantis. Although 1963 was a record setting year for other makes of cars, Studebaker sales plummeted.

Brooks Stevens did another face-lift to create the 1964 models, which looked quite different from the previous year. The roof was again changed and was lowered except on the station wagon and convertible. All front-end sheet metal was new as was the grille. The trunk lid was also new. Model designations were changed. The lowest level Challenger model was added, and for the next level, the Commander name was revived. The Daytona was now available as a 4-door and remained as a station wagon, hardtop, or convertible. The 4-door Cruiser remained.

None of the 1964 Studebakers bore the name "Lark," and it was only mentioned in the literature for the lower priced models. However, these cars are all commonly known as Larks from 1959 through 1966, and I will continue to do so in this book.

Raymond Loewy's team, which had designed the Avanti, was working on a new design that was intended to replace the Lark. The car was unofficially called the "Avanti II." The design strongly resembled the Avanti and included a 4-door fastback, notchback, convertible, and station wagon.

Despite the new look in 1964, which most considered quite pleasing, sales got off to a slow start for the 1964 model year. The announcement was made on Monday, December 9, 1963, that the South Bend factory would shut down and that only the Hamilton plant in Ontario, Canada, would continue to assemble Studebakers. Only Larks would continue to be built and the Avanti, Hawk, and truck models would all be discontinued. The last South Bend-built Lark finished being assembled on December 20, 1963. It was a Bordeaux Red Daytona hardtop with an Avanti R-1 engine and a 4-speed transmission. Fortunately, this vehicle was not sold but rather was added to the Studebaker vehicle collection. Studebaker eventually gave this collection to the city of South Bend and it is now part of the Studebaker National Museum.

For the remainder of 1964, engines were still manufactured in South Bend and shipped to Canada. Studebaker needed another engine to use for its 1965 model. The Ford 289-cid V-8 was a logical choice since Studebaker had a 289, thus there would be a similarity to the new power plant. Unfortunately, Ford was not willing to cooperate and would not sell its engines to Studebaker. Chevrolet was the next choice and General Motors did agree to sell its engines, manufactured by McKinnon Industries, to Studebaker. In fact, the engines were built in St. Catherines, Ontario, Canada. In 1965, Studebaker used the 190-cid 6-cylinder and the 283-cid V-8.

The hardtop, convertible, and Challenger models were dropped in 1965. Available were the 2- and 4-door sedans and 4-door station wagon. Externally, the 1965 model had only minimal changes. The 2-door sedan was upgraded and was now available as a Daytona model that was referred to as a "sport coupe" and came with a vinyl roof. The Cruiser was now offered with a 6-cylinder engine.

The Chevrolet engine performed well in the Studebakers. These engines were lighter and gave the car a different feel. Sales for 1965 were not good, but no one really expected them to be.

In 1966, the grille was modified and the taillights were changed. Body side moldings were lowered. The Chevrolet 230-cid 6-cylinder engine became available. Interiors were upgraded over previous models. Studebaker advertised these cars as "The Common Sense Cars," and they were. They were practical, well built, and economical to operate. However, this wasn't enough. Although the automotive division was showing a profit at the time, the Board of Directors announced in February of 1966 that production would cease. There would be no more Studebakers. The last car rolled off of the line March 16, 1966. It was a green Cruiser that was used as an executive car for a short time and is now on display at the Studebaker National Museum in South Bend, Indiana.

Studebaker had a long history of distinguished vehicles. Lark models have continued to gain popularity with collectors. They're good-looking, fun to drive, some are sporty, and some are even fast. The cars are also reasonably priced and parts generally are plentiful. Harold Churchill's dream of the Lark saving Studebaker didn't happen, but at least it helped prolong the automaker's life.

The clay proposal on the left for either 1957 or 1958 looked very much like what was to become the 1959 Lark in a much shorter and more refined version. The decision to build a smaller car for 1959 was not made until late in 1957.

By 1958, the Bob Bourke–designed 1953 sedan had received many facelifts. The addition of fins and dual headlamps was an attempt to keep up with other automakers at a minimum cost. Sales were not good in the recession year of 1958 and management was patiently waiting for the introduction of its new compact car due in the fall of 1958.

Before making the decision to produce a smaller car for 1959, various facelifts of the 1958 design were explored. The design on the left was accepted. The 1957 Plymouth on the right was used for comparison purposes. Studebaker frequently purchased competitive makes of cars for testing and evaluation.

The 1959 Lark Regal 4-door came with a chrome grille outer ring, chrome headlamp rims, stainless trim around the windows and doors, and a plastic/chrome rim around the taillight lenses. This early prototype was missing the bird grille emblem and front fender "Studebaker" script that were used in production.

The grille emblem was shared with the Hawk in 1959 and was chrome with a black background. Studebaker called it a "corporate emblem." The leftover 1959 Silver Hawk plastic horn center emblem was a similar design. Front and rear bumper guards were optional.

Only solid colors were offered although dealers frequently painted accent colors on the roof as was done on this prototype. Missing are the "Studebaker" and "Lark VI" or "VIII" script from across the rear panel that were used in production. The gas filler was on the rear panel. Chrome plastic rings around the taillight lenses were unique to Regal models.

The Lark Deluxe 2-door sedan was offered only as a 6-cylinder in 1959. Full wheel covers as well as whitewall tires were optional. Studebaker returned to using 15-inch wheels in 1959 and all wheels were painted body color in 1959 and 1960. Lark bumpers were interchangeable from front to back. Deluxe models came with painted headlamp rims and without the grille outer chrome moulding. Windshields did not have stainless trim.

The Detroit skyline provides a background for the new Lark hardtop with its distinctive new roof. The hardtop was available only as a Regal model with either a 170-cid 6-cylinder or 259-cid V-8 engine.

The "Lark VI" or "VIII" script is missing on the right rear panel of this prototype. A Carter WCFB 4-bbl carburetor and dual exhausts were optional on V-8s, which raised horsepower from 180 to 195.

A 2-door was the only station wagon model offered in 1959. This Deluxe model has optional stainless trim around the windshield and back glass. The center section of the side glass slides rearward for ventilation.

The station wagon used a split tailgate with upper and lower hinges. The rear seat folded down to increase carrying space. The rear floorboard panel lifted to access the spare tire and jack. The gas filler was on the left rear fender on station wagons.

A rear-facing third seat that would hold two small passengers was optional. The seat would fold flat when additional cargo space was desired. Station wagons equipped with the third seat option had no spare tire. Instead, "Captive-Air" tires were installed which had an inner lining that, in the event of a puncture, would allow the car to be driven up to 100 miles.

Probably a carryover from the old businessman coupe was the "Panel-wagon." This option was aimed at the salesman or small business that maintained a vehicle for both personal and business use. The Masonite panels were painted body color and clipped over the rear side windows for easy installation and removal.

Studebaker went after the fleet market in 1959 and sold many taxicabs. A special model was offered that was 4.5 inches longer than the standard 4-door Lark. The extra space offered additional rear passenger legroom. In fact, Studebaker boasted that its Lark taxi had more rear seat legroom than a Cadillac.

Lark trunks were small and required heavy suitcases or boxes to be lifted over the rear panel. The spare tire lay flat and the wheel was covered with a cardboard panel. The jack rode on the right side of the trunk. The floor of the trunk was covered with a fiber cover.

Freeman-Spicer, the largest volume Studebaker dealer, was located in South Bend, Indiana, just a block away from the factory. This building is now the home of the Studebaker National Museum and is open to the public.

The 1959 Lark dashboard was a revised version of the 1956–1958 sedan dash. The upper portion on Regal models had vinyl stretched over a thin layer of foam. It looked good but would not have survived any crash test. Regal dashes also had a lower padded rail. The radio speaker was behind the mesh on the right side of the dash. On models equipped with a clock, the speaker was recessed to allow room for the clock. Unfortunately, the passenger was blasted with sound from the speaker as the driver turned the volume loud enough to hear. Pedals continued to go through the floorboard as on earlier models.

Reclining seats, an American Motors favorite, became optional on Studebakers in 1959 and continued through 1966. Regal models had vertical pleats sewn into the cloth or optional vinyl seats. The interiors were very attractive.

Regal model door panels used chrome Mylar inserts with vinyl and cloth on cars equipped with cloth seats. Power windows and seats were not available on Larks.

Deluxe models had plainer solid vinyl door panels. Window crank handles had black knobs from 1959 to 1961. The Deluxe instrument knobs were black in 1959, and all knobs on all 1961 models were black. Regal models used leftover Packard chrome instrument knobs in 1959 and 1960.

Studebaker advertised that the new Lark would comfortably seat six adults. The comparison to the Cadillac was to illustrate the outside size difference along with maintaining the interior space. Tall adults could comfortably drive the new Lark and flat floors provided for easy accessibility.

The Lark chassis was a cut down version of the 1958 chassis along with the same suspension, brakes, engines, and differential.

The 6-cylinder engine was dropped from 185 cid to 170 cid in 1959 in an attempt to squeeze better gas mileage from the 6-cylinder engine. In some tests the 259-cid V-8 got better gas mileage than the 6-cylinder.

The compression ration was raised from 7.8:1 to 8.3:1. Studebaker advertised the Lark as being economical to operate; with an automatic transmission, a Lark averaged 22.44 mpg in the Mobilgas Economy Run.

The 259 was the only V-8 engine offered in the Lark in 1959 and 1960. Engines and transmissions were painted silver from 1959 to 1961. Air cleaners, starters, generators, fans, and valve covers were painted glossy black except in 1961 when valve covers were painted reddish orange. Both dry and oil bath type air cleaners were used and both had decals on the side.

Oil filters were optional until mid-1962 and the mounting bracket attached to the holes on the oil filler located on the front upper section of the engine. The filters were partial flow type and did not filter all of the oil.

The overdrive transmission was a popular option for many years and provided increased fuel economy for both 6-cylinder and V-8 engines by lowering the RPM about 30 percent. The brake master cylinder, which mounted below the floorboard, was continued until 1961 when it was moved up to the firewall. The valve mounted on the frame rail to the right of the master cylinder is the "hill holder." Available only on standard transmission cars, this valve kept the car from rolling backward while on an incline, allowing the driver to take his foot off of the brake pedal to operate the clutch. Disengaging the clutch released the valve and the brake.

Continental made a rear tire kit for the 1959 Lark that was offered by the factory to Studebaker dealers. Although it was a popular option on Ramblers, few Studebakers were ordered with the accessory. The tire assembly tilted rearward to allow access to the fuel filler.

Studebaker was happy with the success of the 1959 Lark and made few changes in the 1960 model. The grille mesh was changed slightly and a newly designed chrome emblem with red background was placed in the lower center. The mesh in the side grilles now matched the center grille. The taillight lenses were changed; the squared corners and the chrome edge were omitted. The stainless side trim was slightly changed where it bent upward on the rear door. Instead of a pointed bend, it now was curved.

The “Studebaker” nameplate on the side of the front fenders was left off in 1960 and replaced by “Lark VI” or Lark VIII,” depending on the engine. The base price for a 1960 6-cylinder hardtop was $2,296 and for a V-8 was $2,431. All models could now be ordered with either a 6-cylinder or V-8 engine.

The first Studebaker convertible since 1952 was introduced in 1960. Available only as a Regal model, the convertible used a special "X" member on the center of the frame and heavy weights behind the front bumper to eliminate shake. A hydraulic power–operated top was standard and was available in black or white pinpoint vinyl. Studebaker-Packard vice president in charge of marketing, Lou Minkel, stands beside the new vehicle, which is parked in front of the Administration Building in South Bend.

Twenty auto dealers from Switzerland inspect a new Lark convertible at the doll-up line at the end of the assembly line in South Bend. The group toured automotive manufacturing plants in the United States.

The 4-door station wagon was reintroduced in 1960. The tailgate area was redesigned with a new lighter upper glass assembly. The new Lark emblem used on the grille was also placed on the tailgate.

A 2-door wagon continued to be offered but only as a Deluxe model. The bar separating the rear side windows was taken off and the front glass section continued to slide rearward for ventilation.

Interiors were pretty much the same in 1960 except that the upper dashboard on Regal models now had pleats sewn into the vinyl. Split individually adjusting front seats along with headrests became optional on Regal models, and padded vinyl sunvisors continued as an option.

Studebaker occasionally did crash tests and engineers inspect this 1960 Lark 4-door, which was intentionally rolled over at its Proving Ground test facility located west of South Bend.

A company in Eau Claire, Michigan, produced the "Larkette." The gasoline-powered, fiberglass-bodied miniature of the Lark was offered to Studebaker dealers to enhance sales.

The Champ pickup was introduced in 1960. Although not really a Lark, it shared the forward body section with the 1959–1960 Lark and was often referred to as the "Lark pickup." Underneath, the pickup chassis was almost identical to what Studebaker had been using since 1949.

The 1961 model Lark didn't look that different but it was actually quite different from the previous model including all of the external sheet metal and the instrument panel. The body height was lowered 1 inch. It was advertised as "The 1961 Lark with Performability."

A new "Skytop" sunroof was offered for all Larks except the station wagon. This folding vinyl top continued as an option through 1963 and was available with black or white pinpoint vinyl.

The taillight lenses had plastic/chrome around the side and edges. Chrome script on the front fenders and rear panel continued to identify the engine. Wheels were all painted silver in 1961.

Deluxe models came with single headlamps and the parking lamps were placed between the headlamp and the grille. The grille outer chrome ring was left off of Deluxe models as had been done in 1959–1960. The grille emblem was the same as used in 1960 except that the background was now painted flat black.

Regal models came with dual headlamps with the parking lamps placed below. The grille outer ring had a painted black line to separate the ring from the mesh. Front and rear vertical bumper guards were optional.

Larks had a new roofline in 1961. The 2-door sedan model was available only as a Deluxe model in all 1959–1961 Larks and the V-8 engine was an option in 1960–1961. All Larks came with small hubcaps and full wheel covers were optional.

The 1961 Lark 2-door hardtop continued as only a Regal model with either the 170-cid 6-cylinder or 259-cid V-8 engine. Stainless rocker panel moldings were added on all Regal models.

A front sway bar that improved cornering was made standard equipment on all 6-cylinder as well as V-8 Larks in 1961. The fluid filler for automatic transmission–equipped cars was moved from the interior floorboard hump to the engine compartment. Air conditioning was now available on all Larks except convertibles.

An optional roof rack enhances this Regal 4-door station wagon. Power steering and power-assisted brakes were available on all Larks from 1959 to 1966.

The 2-door station wagon continued to be offered only as a Deluxe model. Hoods on 1961 Larks were now counterbalanced and did not require a rod to hold open as on previous models. Brake and clutch pedals were suspended in 1961 although the gas pedal still linked through the floorboard. The brake master cylinder attached to the firewall above the steering column.

Engineering considered a spring-loaded folding convertible top, which worked easily by hand, but rejected the proposal in favor of a power hydraulic-operated top.

With the extra frame "X" member and front weights, the convertible was not a light car. The V-8 model weighed in at 3,315 pounds. It was the heaviest model Studebaker.

The 1961 Cruiser was a new top-of-the-line 4-door sedan. The name came from the Land Cruiser, which was a popular Studebaker name used until 1954. The body was the same as that used since 1959 on taxicabs and was 4.5 inches longer than the standard 108.5 4-door Lark.

The Cruiser now came with a V-8 but for the first time the 289-cid was offered as an option. The rear-quarter windows open for ventilation for rear seat passengers.

Cruiser models had plush interiors with center-mounted rear armrests. Map pockets were placed in all of the door panels. All Regal and Cruiser models with cloth seats had small Lark emblems woven into the material.

The instrument panel was new in 1961 and for the first time it was safety padded on top in all Larks. Regal models had ribs in the padding and Deluxe models were smooth. The radio speaker was moved to the top center of the dash and the glove box was moved to the right side. The area surrounding the Stewart Warner instruments and the glove box lid was painted white.

Regal interiors were very attractive. Vinyl seats were standard on convertibles and optional on all other models. Optional split front seats allowed individual adjustment and allowed the passenger to fully recline the seat without affecting the adjustment of the driver's seat. Front and rear floor carpeting was standard on Regal models.

Deluxe interiors were attractive, but much plainer than Regal models. Rear armrests were optional as well as a right side sunvisor. Floorboards were covered with molded rubber mats.

Spare tires had a sewn cover hiding them in 1961 that matched the fiber trunk mat. The trunk area remained small with the spare tire taking much of the space.

New for 1961 was an overhead valve engine called the Skybolt Six. Actually, it was a redesign of the old Champion L-head engine and was expected to give better performance and more miles per gallon.

Engines continued to be painted silver in 1961 but valve covers were painted a reddish orange. Beginning in 1959 all Larks had internally controlled hood releases. In 1961, heater cores were moved from the left inner fender to under the dashboard and the control valve was mounted on the firewall. A filter for the heater slid through a slot on the left side of the firewall.

Oil filters continued to be optional in 1961 but used a screw-on canister rather than the old can with a removable cartridge. Models equipped with power brake boosters had them mounted on the firewall behind the master cylinder. Windshield washer reservoirs of both the bottle and bag type were used in 1961. Missing on this prototype is a decal on the shield above the radiator cap stating “Caution Fan.”

For 1962, Studebaker styling, headed by Randy Faurot, had proposals for two entirely new cars. One was to be on a 100-inch wheelbase and to be powered by a water-cooled, horizontally opposed 139-cid 4-cylinder engine. An original prototype of this engine is on display at the Studebaker National Museum located in South Bend, Indiana. The headlamp rims appear to be from a 1959–1960 Lark and parking lights are from a 1961 Lark Deluxe.

Doors on the smaller car would interchange with the larger Lark. The roof, glass, and bumpers were also shared to cut costs.

The Lark was to continue on the 108.5-inch wheelbase with the same chassis and running gear as before.

Although a lot of money was spent on this new project, it was stopped when Sherwood Egbert took over as Studebaker-Packard president in January 1961. Egbert hired his friend Milwaukee industrial designer Brooks Stevens to redesign the Lark for 1962.

Stevens changed almost all of the exterior sheet metal except for the front doors. The Regal 4-door now used the 112-inch wheelbase chassis, as did the Cruiser and station wagon. Overall length was increased by 13 inches on the 4-door sedan and 9 inches on the Cruiser. The 2-door sedan, hardtop and convertible increased 9 inches. Dual headlamps were now standard on all models and a gold Lark emblem was placed on the lower left corner of the grille.

Block letters now spelled out "Studebaker" across the trunk lid and a "V-8" or "V-S" emblem, similar to those used from 1953 to 1955, was placed on top of the lid. A new hood ornament was standard on all Regal models. Block "Lark" letters were on the front edge of the front fenders. Studebaker advertised the Lark as "the one car that offers big car comfort at compact prices."

In 1962, there were few external differences between Deluxe and Regal models. Hubcap and wheel cover centers were painted red and the wheel covers had outer slots painted white. Wheels were painted off-white on 1962 and later Larks. The 2-door models continued to be offered only with Deluxe trim.

The hardtop and convertible were now offered as Regal or Daytona models. Pictured is a Regal hardtop. All models available with a V-8 engine could now be ordered with the 289-cid engine.

The Daytona hardtop or convertible had slightly different side moldings and a gold "Daytona" script was attached just behind the door. Daytonas came with bucket seats and a center console. A 4-speed floor-mounted transmission was available only on the Daytona.

Stevens gave the car a Mercedes-like grille which extended forward of the headlamps. Bumpers were the same as in 1961 but wrap-around extensions became standard on the Cruiser and optional on other models. Both 2-door and 4-door station wagons continued to be offered.

This Regal convertible was available with a 6-cylinder, 259- or 289-cid V-8. Bench seats were standard on the Regal.

A Lark Daytona convertible paced the Indianapolis 500 Mile Race in May of 1962. Standing behind the car on the left is Indianapolis Studebaker dealer Charlie Stuart, Indianapolis Speedway president Tony Hulman, and Studebaker president Sherwood Egbert.

The Daytona proudly leads the pack of cars beginning the 46th running of the Indianapolis 500. Studebaker brought a couple of Avanti prototypes to the event and referred to the Avanti as the "honorary pace car."

Studebaker sponsored *Mister Ed* on television from 1961 until 1963. It was the first company to put the show on the air and was the first corporation to cosponsor a TV show with its dealers. Participating dealers paid $25.00 for each car sold to help pay for the weekly show. Many Studebakers appeared in the program, which starred Alan Young and Connie Hines.

The 1962 dashboard was similar to the 1961 model but Daytonas and Cruisers were covered with wood graining and a padded extension surrounding the radio. Another padded rail stretched across the lower section of the dash. The ribbed padding on top of the dash was used on all models. Oval steering wheels were used on all Larks from 1961 to 1966. The center cap on the steering wheel contained a clear lens covering a small Lark emblem. Transistor radios became standard in 1962 along with seatbelt anchors mounted in the floorboard for easy seatbelt installation. Seatbelts were still optional and were not made standard until 1963.

Daytona hardtops came with cloth seats and vinyl was optional. Vinyl was standard on convertibles. The vinyl came with electropleated seams. An ashtray was in the center console as well as in the dash. Bucket seats could be ordered with reclining backs and with headrests.

Regal interiors were also finished nicely. Unfortunately, 1962 interiors did not hold up well. The electropleated seams on vinyl equipped cars split, and the foam used under the nylon material on cloth seats turned to powder after a few hot summers.

Studebaker had sales outlets as well as assembly plants located around the world. Champion Motors had this attractive showroom in Adelaide, Australia. Australian Larks were assembled in Melbourne and were right-hand drive.

Fleet sales were always sought and this dealership is making a delivery of 131 Larks to the State of Indiana.

Studebaker called its police car the Marshall. This photo showed the typical police equipment that could be carried in the trunk. The factory claimed 16 cubic feet of trunk space. The trunk mat used in 1962 and later Larks was a hound's-tooth pattern on a rubber mat.

In mid-1962, the oil filter was moved to the lower right side of the engine on both 6-cylinder and V-8 models and became a full-flow filter. The oil filler was moved from the front center of the engine to the valve covers. The valve covers were now retained by two nuts instead of four. The design of the valve cover gasket also changed.

This early 1963 Cruiser prototype has parking lamps above the headlights, a Hawk style red/white/blue grille emblem, body color accents on the wheel covers, and a Hawk style aluminum rocker panel. None of the changes made it into production.

A new roof and non-wraparound windshield were the major changes in 1963. Other changes included new grille mesh, amber parking light lenses, and a new grille emblem with a small Lark emblem on 6-cylinder models and a small "8" on V-8 models. Windshield wipers now swept across the windshield in the same direction for better coverage.

New moldings stretched across the back of the car along with new back-up lamps. Taillight lenses were slightly changed. A new plastic emblem was placed on top of the deck lid with a Lark emblem on 6-cylinder models and a "V-8" on 8-cylinder models. Wheel covers had off-white inserts. A new Prestolite alternator replaced the generator used on previous models.

The Skytop option continued through 1963, although few cars were sold with this option. Avanti engines were optional on Larks in 1963 in either supercharged or nonsupercharged versions. Front disc brakes were also optional.

New models were added in 1963. Bottom of the line (until midyear when the Standard was introduced) was the Regal, which is shown. The Regal came as a 2-door sedan, 4-door sedan, and station wagon. Next was the Custom series, which was available in the same body styles as the Regal. The Daytona continued and now was the only model available for the convertible and hardtop; it was also available as a station wagon. The Cruiser continued as the top-of-the-line 4-door sedan.

The station wagon received the greatest amount of change in 1963. Brooks Stevens sold to Studebaker his patented idea for a sliding rear roof section that would allow tall items to be carried and would allow easier loading and unloading. The new sliding-roof station wagon was called the Wagonaire and came as standard equipment on all models. Station wagons now had a manual roll-up rear window with optional electric operation. The 2-door station wagon was no longer offered.

The Standard model was added mid-year in 1963 and advertised for "budget-minded buyers." The stripped down Lark sold for around $2,000 and was reminiscent of the Scotsman, which was a sales success for Studebaker in 1957–1958.

Amber parking light lenses were added in 1963 and the Daytona had a new side molding that widened along the rear quarter. Bucket seats were now optional.

Brooks Stevens designed a new dashboard for the 1963 Lark with a folding vanity tray in place of the usual glove box. A mirror folded upward and there was a small compartment for maps, and so forth. An AM/FM radio became an option in mid-1963. Three pods contained instruments for the driver. On the left were direct reading gauges for the alternator, temperature, oil pressure, and fuel. In the center was space for an optional clock or tachometer in Avanti-powered models. The speedometer was on the right. A similar setup was used in 1964 although the speedometer was moved to the center. Switches were a rocker-type as used on the Avanti.

The Wagonaire received little attention at the Chicago Auto Show as the new Avanti attracted the crowds. The Avanti was intended to help change the image of the corporation and to attract buyers for all model Studebakers.

Raymond Loewy's designers, who had put together the Avanti, worked on a new sedan that was originally planned for introduction mid-year in 1964. The car, which looked similar to the Avanti, was unofficially called the Avanti II and was offered as a fastback, notchback, station wagon, and convertible.

Brooks Stevens made major changes in 1964 to create a new-looking car. The model lineup changed too. The lowest priced car was now called the Challenger, followed by the Commander. The Daytona and Cruiser remained. The Daytona was now available as a 4-door sedan and Daytonas and Cruisers were only available with V-8 engines.

All cars could be ordered with Avanti engines, which were signified by oval fender emblems and a round grille emblem. Supercharged Avanti engines were referred to as "R-2" and nonsupercharged Avanti engines were referred to as "R-1." Wheel covers were new in 1964.

The Commander sedans had thinner side moldings than the Cruiser and plainer interiors. Bumpers now wrapped around and were still interchangeable from front to back. Sedan models were 6 inches longer than 1963 models, and station wagons were 3 inches longer.

Single headlamps were back again in 1964 on Challenger and Commander models although dual headlamps were optional. The 6-cylinder models had "S" emblems on the side of the roof and 8-cylinder models carried a V-8 flag emblem. All models, except for the Challenger, had a new standup "S" Mercedes-style hood ornament.

The Challenger model had a plain interior and no side moldings. Prices started around $2,000. A few Challengers were ordered with Avanti engines.

The Wagonaire sliding roof continued as standard equipment on station wagons. Models ordered with a fixed roof were not called Wagonaires. Daytona side trim was similar to the Cruiser except that a heavy black line was painted in the center. Cruisers had two smaller painted lines.

The new 1964 styling made for an attractive convertible. Block "Studebaker" letters stretched across the trunk lid and a parallelogram emblem was on the side of the front fenders on Daytona and Cruiser models.

Studebaker continued to seek fleet car sales. Avanti engines were used to entice police car sales, and a few cars were even given to various states and cities in an attempt to sell them cars.

This 6-cylinder Commander was among a group of 1964 Studebakers that set 350 records for endurance and speed at the Bonneville Salt Flats in autumn 1963. This car was driven 1,000 miles and averaged better than 100 mph.

Lewis Minkel, president of Studebaker Automotive Sales Corporation, gives the key of a 1964 Cruiser to Commander R. E. Saunders, commanding officer of the South Bend Naval Reserve Training Center. Six new Studebakers were loaned to the Navy for transporting Navy VIPs attending the football game between Navy and Notre Dame in South Bend.

The dashboard on 1964 model cars was changed around the glove box to allow a newly designed vanity. A small box was located on the bottom of the glove box with a tray that slid out with a folding mirror. The glove box lid also was grooved to hold beverages in place.

A floor-mounted automatic transmission borrowed from the Avanti called the "Powershift" became available in 1963. Cars fitted with Avanti engines had tachometers in the right side of the instrument pod in place of a clock, which was available on other models.

Studebaker announced on December 9, 1963 that automobile production was being shut down in South Bend and all production would be transferred to the Canadian factory in Hamilton, Ontario. Fortunately, a farsighted or perhaps sentimental member of Studebaker management saved the last car produced in South Bend. This Daytona hardtop is now on display at the Studebaker National Museum in South Bend, Indiana.

All automobile production came from the Hamilton, Ontario, plant beginning in January 1964. Shaking hands over the first Canadian-built car for shipment to the United States is Automotive Division president Gordon Grundy on the left and W. A. Moeser, director of manufacturing, on the right.

Miss Dominion of Canada stands beside this Canadian-built convertible. The "Built by Studebaker Craftsman" windshield decal was placed on all windshields on 1964–1965 Studebakers. Beginning with the shift to Canada, the Challenger model was dropped and the Cruiser and Daytona models were now available with 6-cylinder engines. Dual headlamps were standard on all cars.

The Canadian-built 1964 cars continued to be fitted with engines from the South Bend foundry. Hardtop and convertible bodies were still framed in South Bend and shipped to Hamilton for assembly. There were no plans to continue supplying these engines or bodies for more than a few months.

This Daytona convertible with optional wire-type wheel covers is displayed at the Chicago auto show. Avanti engines were no longer available on Canadian-built cars.

Also on display in Chicago was the Novi No. 7 racecar that competed in the Indianapolis 500 race. The car was owned by STP Corporation, a subsidiary of Studebaker.

Before making the decision to move manufacturing to Canada, designs were being worked on for the 1965 model. Subtle changes were planned to make the car appear larger and more refined, which included a modified grille, stainless molding running along the top of the fenders and doors, and redesigned wheel well openings.

The rear section was changed to give the car a wider appearance. The taillight stretched across the back.

The exterior appearance of this 1965 Cruiser is pretty much the same as in 1964 except for the removal of the aluminum trim panel over the rear of the trunk lid. New under the hood was the 190-cid 6-cylinder or 283-cid V-8. Both were supplied by McKinnon Industries, a subsidiary of General Motors.

Hardtops and convertibles were no longer available and the 2-door sedan, now called the "Sport Sedan," was available as a Daytona. Daytona side trim was now identical to the Cruiser. The Daytona now came only as a 2-door sedan or station wagon and was only available with a V-8 engine. A vinyl top in black or white was standard on the 2-door Daytona.

The station wagon continued to include the sliding roof as standard equipment. The Wagonaire was the only model still using the X-member frame. The Commander was offered as a 2- or 4-door sedan or station wagon and was available with a 6-cylinder or V-8 engine. The Cruiser remained as the top-of-the-line 4-door and could be ordered with either engine.

This Commander 2-door participated in the Shell 4,000 Trans-Canada Rally. The car was also displayed at the Chicago Auto Show.

Because of increased engine length, the radiator was moved forward on 6-cylinder models. New engine to frame mounts were required and a new cross member for mounting the transmission was added. Missing from this prototype is a valve cover decal stating "Studebaker Skybolt 190 six" that was used in production.

Studebaker continued to use the same transmission options as in previous years but the floor mounted 4-speed and Powershift automatic were no longer offered. Production models had decals on both valve covers stating "Studebaker Thunderbolt V-8 283."

Minor changes were made to give the 1966 model a different appearance. The grille was new with four rectangular sections. Single headlamps were back for all models. Cruisers and Daytonas had black accents on the headlight rims and grilles, and Commanders did not. The Hawk bird emblem was revived and placed in the center of the wheel covers. The bird emblem was also used in the center of the grille and on each fender along with the displacement of the engine.

The Daytona sport sedan was now available as a 6-cylinder and all 1966 models were available with either a 194-cid or a 230-cid 6-cylinder engine. The 283-cid V-8 continued as an option on all models. The vinyl top was now available as an option on the Cruiser.

The upper portion of the taillight housing was now louvered and used as a passageway for air to leave the passenger compartment thus providing ventilation. This was advertised as the "refreshair circulating system." Taillight lenses were now in the lower part of the housing. Optional backup lamps were attached below the taillights and were the same units that were used on station wagons since 1963.

In 1966, all station wagons were called Wagonaires, even if they did not have the sliding roof. Instead of being standard equipment, the sliding roof was now an extra-cost option.

The 1966 interiors were the most plush of any Studebaker built. The Canadian based company seemed to be intent upon offering the best value for the money. In addition to the rich interiors, many items were now standard that were previously optional. Among the standard items were padded sunvisors, non-glare wiper arms, dual brake master cylinders, 2-speed electric windshield wipers, windshield washers, dual horns, parking brake warning lights, cigar lighters, foam padded seats, interior light switches on all doors, coat hooks, and front and rear ash trays.

The last Studebaker finished assembly on March 16, 1966. The Timberline Turquoise Cruiser was used as an executive car for a period and is now on display at the Studebaker National Museum in South Bend, Indiana.

When Hamilton production was shut down, plans were already underway for the 1967 model. A new grille was added and the rear bumperettes were moved to the front. The 1964 Daytona side molding was returned and placed slightly lower along the side of the body. The rear bumper was raised and a new molding was added to the lower roofline.

Studebaker of Canada hired Marcks, Hazelquist, Powers, Inc., a Dearborn, Michigan, design firm, to make some long range styling proposals. It is doubtful that even if sales were good that the limited production capabilities of the Canadian factory would have produced enough revenue to produce an entirely new car.

The designs showed no resemblance to previous Studebakers other than the bird emblems used on the hood and wheel covers.

Brooks Stevens began making some long-range design proposals soon after being hired by Sherwood Egbert in 1961 to redesign the 1962 Larks and Hawks. Three prototypes were built in Italy. The first was this station wagon, which was originally planned as a 1964 model and shows a resemblance to what was actually produced in 1964. The suicide doors in the back were diagonally interchangeable with the front.

The second Stevens prototype was a 4-door hardtop and was designated for 1965. It had suicide doors in the back, and there was no post when the doors were opened. Doors cut into the roofline to ease entry and exit.

Stevens's third prototype was called the Sceptre and was projected for 1966 or 1967 production. The one-piece headlamp stretched across the front of the car and was specially designed by Sylvania. Polarized glass was used in the rear side section of the roof for increased visibility. The sleek design continues to look contemporary after many years. All three of the Stevens prototypes were built on Lark chassis and all are now part of the Studebaker National Museum in South Bend, Indiana.